Crafty Critters

With a little simple sewing, you can fill your life with fun woodland companions!
These foxes, raccoons, owls, and other critters make captivating accessories.

Meet the Designer

Vickie Clontz is an award-winning designer, teacher, and fiber artist specializing in wool and all things related. She has been sewing since her mother first introduced her to needle and thread at age 5. Her pattern company, Annie's Keepsakes, has close to 100 original designs for sewing, quilting, home decor, and wearables.

Vickie especially loves creating unique designs and finds much inspiration in nature and the countryside. She also enjoys sharing her ideas, talent, and expertise with others through the workshops, programs, and classes she teaches across the country. For more about Vickie and her work, visit her website, annieskeepsakes.com.

Fox & Raccoon Purses 2

Critter Pincushions 6

Fox, Fawn & Skunk Wall Pockets 12

Owl Storage Case 15

Critter Magnets 16

Leaf Mug Rugs 17

Log Storage Case 18

General Instructions 30

LEISURE ARTS, INC. • Maumelle, Arkansas

Fox & Raccoon Purses

Finished Size: 10"w x 8"h

Please read the General Instructions, pages 30-32, before beginning your project.

||||||||||||||||||||||||||||||||||||||||||||||||||||||| SHOPPING LIST |||||||||||||||||||||||||||||||||||||||||||||||||||||||

For each Purse:
- ☐ ¹/₂ yard of cotton fabric for purse lining
- ☐ 1¹/₄ yards of 15" wide fusible interfacing
- ☐ black ⁷/₈" diameter button for nose
- ☐ basic supplies (scissors, straight pins, pencil, hand sewing needle, embroidery needles, sewing machine, iron and ironing board, pressing cloth, rotary cutter, acrylic rulers and cutting mat)

For the Fox:
- ☐ ¹/₂ yard 57/58" wide wool fabric for purse body
- ☐ ¹/₄ yard 57/58" wide wool fabric for purse strap
- ☐ 12" x 14" piece of winter white wool felt
- ☐ 12" x 14" piece of copper wool felt
- ☐ 6" x 8" piece of fusible web
- ☐ size 5 or 8 pearl cotton - copper
- ☐ 2 black ¹¹/₁₆" diameter buttons for eyes

For the Raccoon:
- ☐ ³/₄ yard wool fabric for purse body
- ☐ 10" x 12" piece of white wool felt
- ☐ 13" x 14" piece of grey wool felt
- ☐ 7" x 10" piece of black wool felt®
- ☐ 3" x 6" piece of paper-back fusible web
- ☐ black and grey size 8 or 5 pearl cotton
- ☐ 2 white ³/₄" diameter buttons for eyes
- ☐ 2 black ⁹/₁₆" diameter buttons for eyes

||||||||||||||||||||||||||||||||||||||||||||||||||||||||||||||||||||||||||||||||||||||||||||||||||||||||||||||||||||||||||||||||||||

CUTTING THE PIECES

*Follow **Rotary Cutting**, page 31, to cut fabrics. All measurements include seam allowances. Follow **Making and Using Patterns**, page 30, to make and use tracing paper **or** freeze paper patterns.*

For the Fox or Raccoon:
From cotton fabric:
- Cut **purse front/back lining** 10¹/₂" x 18".

From fusible interfacing:
- Cut **purse front/back** 10¹/₂" x 18".
- Use pattern, page 21, to cut **flap interfacing**.
- Cut **strap** 2" x 45".

For the Fox:
From wool fabric for purse body:
- Cut **purse front/back** 10¹/₂" x 18".
- Use pattern, page 21, to cut **flap lining**.

From wool fabric for purse strap:
- Cut **strap** 4" x 45".

From winter white wool felt:
- Use pattern, page 21, to cut **flap**.
- Cut **rectangle** 5" x 7".

From copper wool felt:
- Use pattern, page 20, to cut **forehead**.
- Cut **rectangle** 5" x 7".

From fusible web:
- Cut **rectangle** 5" x 7".

For the Raccoon:
From wool fabric for purse body:
- Cut **purse front/back** 10¹/₂" x 18".
- Use pattern, page 21, to cut **flap lining**.
- Cut **strap** 4" x 45".

From white wool felt:
- Use pattern, page 21, to cut **flap**.

From grey wool felt:
- Use pattern, page 20, to cut **forehead**.
- Use pattern, page 20, to cut 4 **outer ears**.

From black wool felt:
- Use pattern, page 20, to cut 2 **masks**.

To make the Purse:

Match right sides and raw edges and use ¼" seam allowances unless otherwise indicated. Backstitch at the beginning and end of seams. Press seam allowances open after sewing each seam unless otherwise indicated.

Making the Flap

1. **For the Fox**, place the **forehead** on the winter white **flap**; pin. Using copper pearl cotton, Blanket Stitch the forehead to the flap.

   For the Raccoon, place the **forehead** and **masks** on the winter white **flap**; pin. Using black pearl cotton, Blanket Stitch the mask to the flap. Using grey pearl cotton, Blanket Stitch the forehead to the flap.

2. **For the Fox**, baste sides and upper edge of the forehead close to edges on flap.

   For the Raccoon, baste sides of forehead and mask and upper edge of nose close to edges on flap.

3. **For the Fox**, sew ¹¹/₁₆" buttons to flap for eyes.

   For the Raccoon, stack the small black buttons on the white buttons and sew to flap for eyes.

4. Fuse **interfacing flap** to wool fabric **flap lining**. Sew the flap and flap lining together along sides and bottom edge. Trim lining seam allowance slightly; clip curves. Turn the flap right side out; press. Baste upper straight edges together close to edge.

Adding the Ears

1. **For the Fox**, follow manufacturer's instructions and use fusible web to fuse the winter white and copper wool felt **rectangles** together. Use pattern, page 20, to cut 1 ear; cut 1 ear in reverse. With winter white on top, fold the top edge of the ear on fold line and gently steam. Baste lower edges together. Repeat for remaining ear.

   For the Raccoon, trace one inner ear and one inner ear in reverse onto paper-back fusible web. Fuse web to black felt; cut out inner ears. To make ear front, fuse each inner ear to an outer ear. Zigzag stitch around each inner ear. Sew one ear front to one ear; clip curves and turn right side out. Repeat for remaining ear.

2. Baste ears, right side down, to flap front about ¼" from side edge.

Making the Purse Body and Lining

1. Fuse **interfacing purse front/back** to wool fabric **purse front/back**.

2. Matching right sides, fold the wool purse front/back in half to measure 10½" x 9". Sew the sides together.

3. To box the lower corner of the purse body, match the right sides and center the side seam. Use the fabric marking pencil to mark a line perpendicular to the side seam 1" from the point *(Fig. 2)*. Stitch along drawn line. Trim corners of purse ¼" from stitching line. Repeat for remaining corner. Turn purse body right side out. Press front top edge only ½" to the wrong side.

Fig. 2

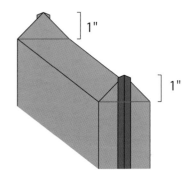

4. Repeat Steps 2-3 with the purse front/back lining; turn right side out. Press top edge ½" to inside.

Adding the Strap

1. Fuse one long edge of the **interfacing strap** to the wrong side of fabric along one long edge of **strap**.

2. Matching right sides and long raw edges, fold strap in half; stitch along long edges, leaving short ends open for turning. Turn the strap right side out; press. Topstitch 1/4" from each long edge.

3. On the right side of the fabric, baste strap ends to the upper edge of the purse back about 1/2" from the side seam.

Assembling the Purse

1. Using a 1/2" seam allowance, baste the right side of the flap to the right side of purse body back along the raw edges with ears and strap sandwiched in between.

2. Place the purse lining inside the purse body. Aligning pressed top edges, whipstitch lining to purse.

3. Sew the button to the purse body for the nose.

4. For the loop closure, cut three 18" lengths of pearl cotton. Secure the threads on one side of the forehead. Braid the lengths together for about 1 3/4". Secure the threads to the other side of the forehead.

Critter Pincushions

Butterfly Wrist Pincushion

Finished Size: 4¼"w x 3"h

Please read the General Instructions on pages 30-32 before beginning your project.

||||||| **SHOPPING LIST** |||||||

- ☐ 6½" x 10" piece of yellow/orange variegated wool felt (or solid yellow wool felt if dyeing your own, see page 30)
- ☐ 4" square of black wool felt
- ☐ 2" square of white wool felt
- ☐ 2" square of copper wool felt
- ☐ 2" square of black cotton fabric
- ☐ 2" x 4" piece of paper-backed fusible web
- ☐ 4" length of black baby rick-rack
- ☐ sewing thread to match yellow/orange wool felt and black
- ☐ size 8 pearl cotton - black
- ☐ liquid fray preventative
- ☐ polyester fiberfill
- ☐ 10" length of ⅜" wide black elastic
- ☐ 1 pkg of orange unsweetened powdered soft drink mix (optional)
- ☐ basic sewing supplies (tape measure, ruler, tracing paper, seam ripper, sewing machine, scissors, freezer paper, hand sewing needle, embroidery needle, iron and ironing board, stuffing tool such as a chopstick)

|||||||||||||||||||||||||||||||||||||||||||||||||

To make the Pincushion:
Match the right sides and raw edges and use a ¼" seam allowance when sewing.

1. Follow **Making and Using Freezer Paper Patterns**, page 30, to use the Butterfly Wrist Pincushion patterns, page 23, to cut the wings from yellow/orange felt. Cut the body and teardrop spots from black felt. Cut a slit (indicated by the red line on the pattern) in *one* wings piece for the wings back.

2. Trace 2 of each round spot pattern, page 23, onto the paper side of the fusible web; cut out about ⅜" away from the drawn lines. Follow the manufacturer's instructions to fuse the web to the white and copper wool felt. Cut out the pieces.

3. Remove the paper backing and fuse the round spots to the teardrop spots.

4. Pin the spots and body to the front wings piece. For the antennae, fold the rick-rack in half and tuck the fold under the top of the body piece. Use pearl cotton to work Blanket Stitches around the body (securely catching the rick-rack in the stitches) and teardrop spots. Trim the antennae as desired and add a drop of fray preventative to the cut ends; allow to dry.

5. Being careful not to catch the body or antennae in the stitching, sew the wings together along the outer edges. Trim the seam allowances to ⅛" and clip the curves. Turn the butterfly right side out through the back opening and press. Stuff the pincushion with fiberfill, using the chopstick to tightly pack fiberfill into the curved outer edges. Hand sew the opening closed.

6. Wrap the elastic around your wrist, overlapping the ends about ¾". Being sure the band will pass over your hand, trim the excess elastic. Securely sew the overlapping ends together.

7. Press two opposite sides of the black fabric square ¼" to the wrong side. Placing the pressed edges at the sides, wrap the fabric several times around the overlapped area of the elastic. Trim any excess fabric and press the raw edge ¼" to the wrong side. Whipstitch in place. Placing the overlapped area of the fabric over the whipstitched area of the pincushion, securely whipstitch the elastic band to the pincushion back.

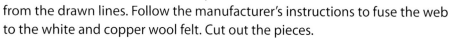

Fox Pincushion

Finished Size: 5^1/$_2$" high

Please read the General Instructions, pages 30-32, before beginning your project.

|||||||||||||||||| **SHOPPING LIST** ||||||||||||||||||

- ☐ 12" x 19" piece of copper wool felt
- ☐ 7" x 8" piece of white wool felt
- ☐ 2" square of black wool felt
- ☐ sewing thread to match copper wool felt and black
- ☐ size 8 pearl cotton - copper, white, and black
- ☐ 2 black ^{5}/$_{16}$" diameter two-hole buttons
- ☐ polyester fiberfill
- ☐ crushed walnut shells
- ☐ basic sewing supplies (tape measure, ruler, sewing machine, scissors, freezer paper, hand sewing needle, embroidery needles, iron and ironing board, stuffing tool such as a chopstick)

To make the Pincushion:

Match the right sides and raw edges and use a ^{1}/$_4$" seam allowance when sewing.

1. Follow **Making and Using Freezer Paper Patterns**, page 30, to use the Fox patterns, pages 21-22, to cut the body, forehead, and tail from rust felt. Cut the face and tail tips from white felt. Cut a nose from black felt. For the bow tie, cut a ^{3}/$_4$" x 2" and a ^{1}/$_2$" x 1" piece of black felt.

2. Pin the face, forehead, and nose to a body, placing the white face ^{1}/$_4$" in from the cut edges and aligning the copper forehead with the white face. Use pearl cotton to work Blanket Stitches around the face, forehead, and nose. Pin one tail tip to each tail. Work Blanket Stitches across the straight edge of each tail tip.

3. For the eyes, sew the buttons to the face. For the bow tie, pinch the larger felt piece in the middle and wrap with the smaller black felt piece; whipstitch small piece in place. Securely hand sew the bow tie to the body.

4. Sew the body pieces together, leaving the bottom edge open. Trim the seam allowances to ^{1}/$_8$" along the ear and cheek areas; clip the curves. Turn the fox right side out and press. Press the bottom edges ^{1}/$_4$" to the wrong side. Firmly stuff the body with fiberfill and hand sew the opening closed.

5. Sew the tail pieces together, leaving the short straight edge open. Trim the seam allowances to ^{1}/$_8$" and clip the curves. Turn the tail right side out and press. Press the short straight edges ^{1}/$_4$" to the wrong side. Stuff the tail with crushed walnut shells and slipstitch the opening closed. Wrap the tail around the bottom of the fox. Securely whipstitch the tail to the body, allowing the fox to stand.

Hedgehog Pincushion

Finished Size: 4¹/₂"w x 3"h

Please read the General Instructions, pages 30-32, before beginning your project.

||||||||||||||||| SHOPPING LIST ||||||||||||||||||

- ☐ 6" x 10" piece of winter white wool felt
- ☐ 5" x 8" piece of heather grey wool felt
- ☐ 3 black 3mm beads
- ☐ sewing thread to match winter white felt
- ☐ size 8 pearl cotton - grey/beige
- ☐ polyester fiberfill
- ☐ crushed walnuts shells
- ☐ 1³/₈" long white round head pins
- ☐ basic supplies (freezer paper, pencil, sewing machine, scissors, hand sewing needles, straight pins, tailor's chalk, iron and ironing board, stuffing tool such as a chopstick)

To make the Pincushion:

Match right sides and raw edges and use a ¹/₄" seam allowance when sewing. Use pearl cotton for all embroidery.

1. Follow **Making and Using Freezer Paper Patterns**, page 30, to use the Hedgehog patterns, page 23, to cut the body and ears from winter white felt. Cut the upper body from heather grey felt.

2. Pin one upper body to each body. Pin one ear to each upper body. Going through all layers and catching the bottom edge of the ear in the stitching, Blanket Stitch along the lower edge of one upper body. Repeat to make a second body.

3. Pin the 2 bodies together. Leaving an opening for turning, sew around the hedgehog. Clip curves and trim points; turn right side out. Use the chopstick to push out curves and corners.

4. Sew black beads to the face for the nose and eyes.

5. Use the chopstick to tightly pack fiberfill into the hedgehog's head, tail area, and upper back. Use a funnel or spoon to finish filling the hedgehog with crushed walnut shells; add a final thin layer of fiberfill. Tuck the seam allowances to the inside and hand sew the opening closed.

6. Insert straight pins in the hedgehog's upper body for "quills".

Raccoon Pincushion

Finished Size: 5½" high

Please read the General Instructions, pages 30-32, before beginning your project.

|||||||||||||||||||| **SHOPPING LIST** ||||||||||||||||||||

- ☐ 8" x 13" piece of heather grey wool felt
- ☐ 8" x 10" piece of grey/black striped wool fabric
- ☐ 3" x 5½" piece of white wool felt
- ☐ 3" x 5½" piece of black wool felt
- ☐ 2" square of red wool felt
- ☐ sewing thread to match grey, black, and red wool felt
- ☐ size 8 pearl cotton - white and black
- ☐ 2 black ⁵⁄₁₆" diameter two-hole buttons
- ☐ 2 green ⁷⁄₁₆" diameter two-hole buttons
- ☐ polyester fiberfill
- ☐ crushed walnut shells
- ☐ basic sewing supplies (tape measure, ruler, sewing machine, scissors, freezer paper, hand sewing needle, embroidery needles, iron and ironing board, stuffing tool such as a chopstick)

To make the Pincushion:

Match the right sides and raw edges and use a ¼" seam allowance when sewing.

1. Follow **Making and Using Freezer Paper Patterns**, page 30, to use the Raccoon patterns, pages 21-22, to cut the body from heather grey felt. Cut the face from white felt. Cut the mask, inner ears and nose from black felt. Cut the tail from grey/black striped fabric. For the bow tie, cut a ¾" x 2" and a ½" x 1" piece of red felt

2. Pin the face, mask, nose, and inner ears to a body piece, placing the face and inner ear pieces ¼" in from the cut edges and aligning the mask with the face. Use pearl cotton to work Blanket Stitches around the white face, black mask, ears, and nose.

3. For the eyes, layer and sew the green and black buttons to the face. For the bow tie, pinch the larger red felt piece in the middle and wrap with the smaller piece; whipstitch in place. Securely hand sew the bow tie to the body.

4. Sew the body pieces together, leaving the bottom edge open. Trim the seam allowances to ⅛" along the ear and cheek areas; clip the curves. Turn the raccoon right side out and press. Press the bottom edges ¼" to the wrong side. Firmly stuff the body with fiberfill and hand sew the opening closed.

5. Sew the tail pieces together, leaving the short straight edge open. Trim the seam allowances to ⅛" and clip the curves. Turn the tail right side out and press. Press the short straight edges ¼" to the wrong side. Stuff the tail with crushed walnut shells and slipstitch the opening closed. Wrap the tail around the bottom of the raccoon. Securely whipstitch the tail to the body, allowing the raccoon to stand.

Owl Pincushion

Finished Size: 5$\frac{1}{2}$" high

Please read the General Instructions, pages 30-32, before beginning your project.

Please read the General Instructions, pages 30-32, before beginning your project.

|||||||||||||||||| SHOPPING LIST ||||||||||||||||||||

- ☐ 8" x 11" piece of heather brown wool felt
- ☐ 3" x 4" piece of brown wool felt
- ☐ 2" square of white wool felt
- ☐ 2" x 3" piece of tan wool felt
- ☐ 2" square paper-backed fusible web
- ☐ sewing thread to match heather brown and white wool felt
- ☐ size 8 pearl cotton - tan and brown
- ☐ 2 white seed beads
- ☐ 2 brown $\frac{3}{8}$" diameter two-hole buttons
- ☐ 2 1$\frac{1}{2}$" wooden stars
- ☐ polyester fiberfill
- ☐ tan acrylic paint and paintbrush
- ☐ hot glue gun and glue sticks
- ☐ basic sewing supplies (tape measure, ruler, sewing machine, scissors, freezer paper, hand sewing needle, embroidery needles, iron and ironing board, and stuffing tool, such as a chopstick)

To make the Pincushion:
Match the right sides and raw edges and use a $\frac{1}{4}$" seam allowance when sewing. Use pearl cotton for all embroidery.

1. Follow **Making and Using Freezer Paper Patterns**, page 30, to use the Owl patterns, page 24, to cut the body from heather brown felt. Cut the beak from tan felt. Cut the tummy circle and large eye circles from brown felt.

2. Trace the small eye circles onto the paper side of the fusible web. Cut out the circles just outside the drawn lines. Follow the manufacturer's instructions to fuse the small eye circle patterns to the white felt. Cut out the pieces.

3. Remove the paper backing and fuse the white eye circles to the brown eye circles. Pin the facial features and tummy to a body piece. Use pearl cotton to work Blanket Stitches around the brown eyes and beak. Work Straight Stitches and Cross Stitches on the tummy circle.

4. Sew the buttons to the eyes. Use white thread to sew the seed beads to the eyes over the buttons.

5. Sew the body pieces together, leaving the bottom edge open. Trim the seam allowances to $\frac{1}{8}$" along the ear and cheek areas; clip the curves. Turn the owl right side out and press. Press the bottom edges $\frac{1}{4}$" to the wrong side. Firmly stuff the body with fiberfill and hand sew the opening closed.

6. Paint the stars tan; allow to dry. Placing the stars so that the owl will stand, hot glue the stars to the bottom of the owl.

Fox, Fawn & Skunk Wall Pockets

Finished Size: 6½" x 6½" (excluding ears)

Please read the General Instructions, pages 30-32, before beginning your project.

SHOPPING LIST

For the Fox Wall Pocket

- ☐ 8" x 12" piece of white wool felt for head front and ears
- ☐ 8" x 16" piece of rust wool felt for head back, forehead, and ears
- ☐ 2" x 3" piece of black wool felt for nose
- ☐ 18" length of ⅛" wide rust satin ribbon
- ☐ size 5 pearl cotton - black and rust
- ☐ 2 black ½" diameter buttons
- ☐ 3" x 7" piece of fusible web

For the Fawn Wall Pocket

- ☐ 8" x 12" piece of cream wool felt for head front, spots, and ears
- ☐ 8" x 16" piece of tan wool felt for head back, forehead and ears
- ☐ 2" x 3" piece of black wool felt for nose
- ☐ 3" x 3" piece of white wool felt for spots
- ☐ 18" length of ⅛" wide tan suede lacing
- ☐ size 5 pearl cotton - black and tan
- ☐ 2 black ½" diameter buttons
- ☐ 3" x 7" and 3" x 3" pieces of fusible web

For the Skunk Wall Pocket

- ☐ 12" x 18" piece of black wool felt for ears, head front, and head back
- ☐ 6" x 6" piece of white wool felt for stripe and hair
- ☐ 4" x 6" piece of pink wool felt for nose and inner ears
- ☐ 18" length of ⅜" wide black grosgrain ribbon
- ☐ size 5 pearl cotton - white and pink
- ☐ 2 black ½" diameter buttons
- ☐ 2 green ¾" diameter buttons

In addition to the supplies listed above, you will also need:

- ☐ general-purpose sewing thread to match felt
- ☐ basic supplies (scissors, straight pins, pencil, hand sewing needle, embroidery needles, sewing machine, iron and ironing board, pressing cloth)

To make the Fox Wall Pocket:

Match right sides and raw edges and use a ¼" seam allowance when sewing. Use pearl cotton for all embroidery.

1. Follow **Making and Using Freezer Paper Patterns**, page 30, to use the Fox Wall Pocket patterns, pages 24-25, to cut the head front from white felt. Cut the head back and forehead from rust felt. Cut the nose from black felt.

2. From white wool felt, cut a 3" x 7" rectangle. From rust wool felt, cut a 3" x 7" rectangle.

3. Follow the manufacturer's instructions to fuse the rust and white rectangles together. From fused rectangle, use the ear pattern, page 24, to cut 1 ear and 1 ear reversed. With the white side facing, fold ear where indicated on pattern; lightly press. Stitch across the ear, close to bottom edge, to secure fold. Repeat for remaining ear.

4. Matching top and side raw edges, pin the forehead to the head. Blanket Stitch the curved edges of the forehead to the head.

5. Matching bottom raw edges and overlapping bottom edge of head front, pin nose in place. Blanket Stitch across the top edge only of the nose.

6. Sew the buttons to the head front for eyes.

7. Matching right sides, sew the head front and head back together. Clip curves and turn right side out; press. Tuck the ear and ear reversed between the top edges of the forehead and head front, close to the side seams; pin. Working through all layers, Blanket Stitch around the top edge.

8. Tie a knot about 1/2" from each ribbon end. Securely hand sew the ribbon ends to the inside seams of the wall pocket.

To make the Fawn Wall Pocket:
Match right sides and raw edges and use a 1/4" seam allowance when sewing. Use pearl cotton for all embroidery.

1. Follow **Making and Using Freezer Paper Patterns**, page 30, to use the Fawn Wall Pocket patterns, pages 24-25, to cut the head front from cream felt. Cut the head back and forehead from tan felt. Cut the nose from black felt.

2. From cream wool felt, cut a 3" x 7" rectangle. From tan wool felt, cut a 3" x 7" rectangle.

3. Using the tan and cream 3" x 7" rectangles, the head front and head back, follow Steps 3-5 of **Fox Wall Pocket**.

4. From white wool felt, cut a 3"x 3" square. Trace the Spots patterns, page 25, onto the paper side of the fusible web square. Follow manufacturer's instructions to fuse the web square to the wool felt square. Cut out the spots on the drawn lines.

5. Remove the paper backing and fuse spots to the forehead. Sew the buttons to the head front for eyes. Make Straight Stitch eyelashes.

6. Follow Steps 7-8 of **Fox Wall Pocket**, using suede cord in place of ribbon in Step 8.

To make the Skunk Wall Pocket:
Match right sides and raw edges and use a 1/4" seam allowance when sewing. Use pearl cotton for all embroidery.

1. Follow **Making and Using Freezer Paper Patterns**, page 30, to use the Skunk Wall Pocket patterns, pages 24-25, to cut the ears and head front and back from black felt. Cut the stripe and hair from white felt. Cut the nose and inner ears from pink felt.

2. Matching straight raw edges, Blanket Stitch an inner ear to an outer ear along the curved edge only. Matching right sides, pin and then sew the layered ear and an outer ear together. Clip curves and turn right side out; press. Repeat using remaining inner and outer ears to make 1 ear reversed.

3. Matching top and bottom raw edges, center the white stripe on the head front; pin. Going through both layers, Blanket Stitch the curved edges of the stripe to the head. Center the hair on the stripe and Blanket Stitch across the straight top edge.

4. Matching bottom raw edges and overlapping the bottom edge of the stripe, pin the nose in place. Blanket Stitch along the top edge of the nose.

5. Sew the buttons to the head front for eyes.

6. Matching right sides, pin and then sew the head front and head back together. Clip curves and turn right side out; press. On the top edge, pin the ear and ear reversed close to the side seams. Working through all layers, Blanket Stitch around the top edge.

7. Tie a knot about 1/2" from each ribbon end. Securely hand sew the ribbon ends to the inside seams of the wall pocket.

Owl Storage Case

Keep an eye on your glasses with this cute case!

Finished Size: 4¼"w x 7"h

Please read the General Instructions on pages 30-32 before beginning your project.

||||||||||||||||||||| **SHOPPING LIST** |||||||||||||||||||

- ☐ 7¾" x 9" piece of brown wool felt for case
- ☐ 1" x 2½" strip of brown wool felt for closure loop
- ☐ 5" x 8" piece of heather brown wool felt for forehead
- ☐ 5" x 6" piece of tan wool felt for eyes
- ☐ 2" x 3" piece of dark brown wool felt for pupils
- ☐ 2" x 3" piece of gold wool felt for beak
- ☐ 7¾" x 9" piece of cotton fabric for lining
- ☐ 7¾" x 9" piece of fusible fleece
- ☐ 1¼" long brown toggle button
- ☐ sewing thread to match brown wool felt and white
- ☐ size 8 pearl cotton - dark brown
- ☐ 2 white seed beads
- ☐ basic sewing supplies (tape measure, ruler, tracing paper, seam ripper, sewing machine, scissors, freezer paper, hand sewing needle, embroidery needle, iron and ironing board)

To make the Case:

Match the right sides and raw edges and use a ¼" seam allowance when sewing. Use pearl cotton for all embroidery.

1. Follow **Making and Using Freezer Paper Patterns**, page 30, to use the Owl Case patterns, page 26, to cut the pupils from dark brown felt. Cut the eyes from tan felt. Cut the forehead from heather brown felt an the beak from gold felt.

2. Pin the pupils, eyes, beak and forehead to one short end of the brown felt rectangle. Work Blanket Stitches around the pupils, eyes, forehead, and beak.

3. Fuse the fusible fleece rectangle to the wrong side of the brown felt rectangle. Use white thread to sew the seed beads to the eyes. Matching the short edges, fold the rectangle in half. Sew together along the side and bottom edges; trim across corners. Turn right side out and press. Leaving a 4" opening for turning, sew the lining together in the same manner, but do not turn right side out.

4. For the loop, fold the brown felt strip into thirds along the length. The folded loop should measure about ⅜" x 2½". Use matching thread to stitch through the center with a narrow zigzag stitch. Matching raw edges and placing the ends about 1" apart, pin the loop to the top center back of the case; baste across ends.

5. Matching the right sides, place the case in the lining and sew together along the top edge. Turn the case right side out through the lining opening. Slipstitch the opening closed and insert the lining in the case; press. Sew the button to the top center front of the case.

Critter Magnets

Finished Size: approximately 2" high

IIIIIIIIIII **SHOPPING LIST** IIIIIIIIIII

For each Magnet:

☐ 2 black 3mm beads

☐ posterboard

☐ paper-backed fusible web

☐ ³/4" diameter round magnet

☐ basic supplies (craft glue, tracing paper, pencil, scissors, iron and ironing board; Fawn only, white acrylic paint and a toothpick)

For the Fox, Fawn, Bear, and Owl:

☐ 3" x 6" piece of wool felt for forehead/outer ears

☐ 2" x 2" piece of wool felt for face and inner ears

☐ scraps of wool felt for noses, owl eyes, and owl beak

For the Raccoon:

☐ 3" x 6" piece of grey wool felt for head

☐ 2" x 2" piece of white wool felt for stripe

☐ 2" x 2" piece of back wool felt for mask, inner ears and nose

IIIIIIIIIIIIIIIIIIIIIIIIIIIIIIIIIIIIIIIIIIIIIIIIIIIIII

To make each Magnet:

1. Trace the face pattern for the desired critter, pages 27-29, onto tracing paper; cut out. Draw around the paper circle onto posterboard; cut out.

2. Trace the patterns for the desired critter, pages 27-29, onto the paper side of fusible web; roughly cut apart. Fuse the patterns to the corresponding wool felt pieces. Cut out the pieces and remove the paper backing.

3. For the Fawn, Fox, Bear, and Owl, layer and fuse the pieces in the following order: head back, posterboard face, felt face, and forehead. For the Fawn, Fox, and Bear, fuse the inner ears and nose to the forehead. For the Owl, fuse the eyes and beak on the face.
   For the Raccoon, layer and fuse the pieces in the following order: head back, posterboard face, and head front. Arrange and fuse the stripe, mask, and nose on the head front.

4. Glue the beads to the face for eyes. Glue the magnet to the back. For the Fawn, dip a toothpick in the white paint and add spots on the forehead.

Leaf Mug Rugs

Finished Size: approximately 7"w x 7"h

Please read the General Instructions, pages 30-32, before beginning your project.

|||||||| **SHOPPING LIST** ||||||||

For *each* **Leaf**

☐ 9" x 18" piece of wool felt

☐ 9" x 9" piece of thin batting

☐ 10" length of jute twine

☐ sewing thread to match felt

☐ coordinating variegated thread for topstitching

☐ basic supplies (tracing paper, sewing machine, scissors, hand sewing needles, straight pins, tailor's chalk, iron and ironing board)

||||||||||||||||||||||||||||||||||||||||||||||||

To make *each* **Leaf**
Match right sides and raw edges and use a ¹/₄" seam allowance.

1. Follow **Making and Using Freezer Paper Patterns**, page 30, to use the desired leaf pattern, pages 26-29, to cut a leaf front and leaf back from wool felt. Pin the freezer paper pattern to the batting piece; cut out.

2. Layer the batting leaf, leaf back and leaf front; pin the layers together.

3. Fold the jute length in half and leaving the ends extending about ¹/₂" beyond the raw edges, insert the folded end between the layers at the leaf base.

4. Leaving an opening for turning, sew around the leaf; reinforce the stitching across the jute ends. Leaving jute ends long, trim seam allowances across corners and clip curves. Turn the leaf right side out.

5. Working through the opening, use a blunt object such as a crochet hook or chopstick to push out points and smooth curves. Hand sew opening closed; lightly press.

6. Using the stitching lines on the pattern as a reference, topstitch through all layers to create veins in the leaf.

Log Storage Case

Camouflage your rotary cutter, eyeglasses, or other small items with this wood-grain stitched case!

Finished Size: 3¹/₂"w x 7"h

Please read the General Instructions on pages 30-32 before beginning your project.

SHOPPING LIST

- ☐ 10" square of brown wool felt
- ☐ 1" x 2¹/₂" strip of brown wool felt
- ☐ 6" square of green variegated felted wool (or solid yellow wool felt if dyeing your own, see page 30)
- ☐ 8" x 7³/₄" piece of cotton fabric for lining
- ☐ 10" square of fusible fleece
- ☐ sewing thread to match wool felt
- ☐ tan variegated thread
- ☐ Transfer-Eze® transfer paper
- ☐ 1 pkg each of red and green unsweetened powdered soft drink mix (optional)
- ☐ basic sewing supplies (tape measure, ruler, tracing paper, seam ripper, sewing machine, scissors, hand sewing needle, iron and ironing board)

To make the Case:
Match the right sides and raw edges and use a ¹/₄" seam allowance when sewing.

1. Fuse the fleece square to the wrong side of the brown felt square.

2. To make the leaf, trace the pattern on page 20 onto tracing paper; cut out. Use the pattern to cut 2 green wool leaves. Leaving the bottom straight edge of the stem open for turning, sew the leaves together. Trim across the point, clip curves. Turn the leaf right side out; press.

3. Follow the manufacturer's instructions to photocopy the woodgrain, page 19, and leaf, page 20, stitching patterns onto the transfer paper. Adhere the patterns to the leaf and to the center of the brown wool square.

4. For the woodgrain stitching, use the tan variegated thread and start at the pink dot and end at the blue dot. Start again at the green dot and end at the orange dot. For the leaf use the tan variegated thread to sew along the drawn lines.

5. Soak the stitched pieces in cold water to remove the Transfer-Eze. Air dry or dry in the dryer on the lowest setting. Gently steam-press to remove any wrinkles.

6. For the loop, fold the brown felt strip into thirds along the length. The folded loop should measure about ³/₈" x 2¹/₂". Stitch along the center using a narrow zigzag stitch.

7. Centering the stitching, trim the brown felt square to 8" x 7³/₄". Matching the short ends, fold the brown wool piece in half. Sew together along the side and bottom edges; trim corners. Turn right side out and press. Leaving a 4" opening for turning, sew the lining together in the same manner, but do not turn right side out.

8. Pin the straight edge of the leaf stem to the top center back of the case; baste in place. Pin the loop to the top center front of the case, placing the ends about 1" apart; baste in place. Matching right sides, place the case in the lining and sew together along the top edge. Turn the case to the right side through the lining opening. Slipstitch the opening closed and insert the lining into the case. Press the holder. Slip the leaf through the loop to close the case.

Top

19

Patterns

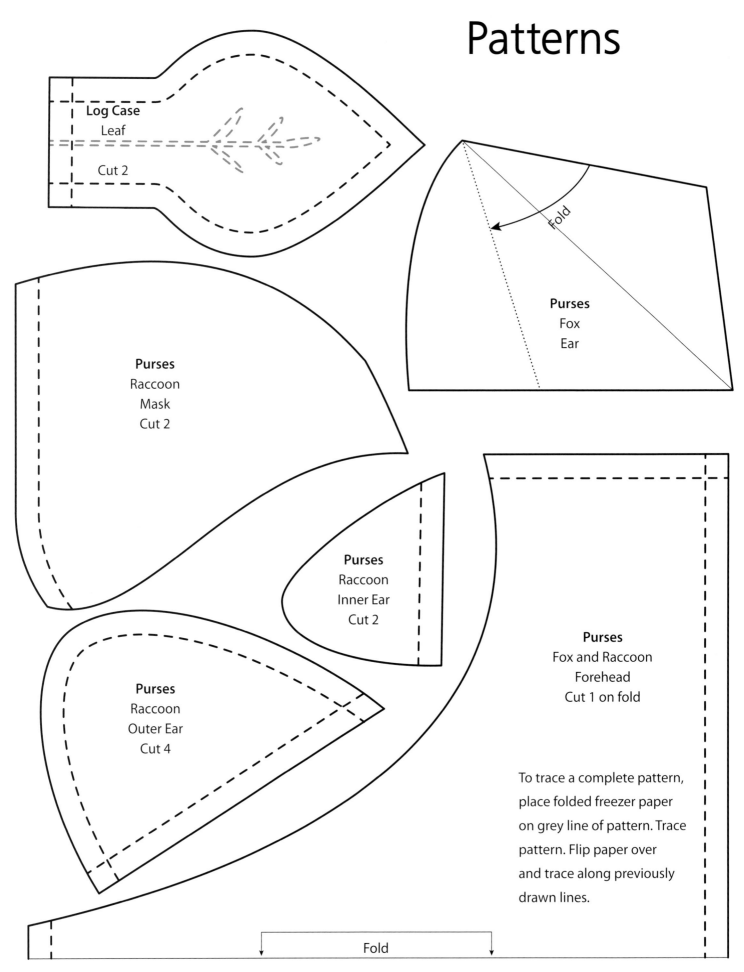

Log Case
Leaf

Cut 2

Purses
Raccoon
Mask
Cut 2

Purses
Fox
Ear

fold

Purses
Raccoon
Inner Ear
Cut 2

Purses
Raccoon
Outer Ear
Cut 4

Purses
Fox and Raccoon
Forehead
Cut 1 on fold

To trace a complete pattern, place folded freezer paper on grey line of pattern. Trace pattern. Flip paper over and trace along previously drawn lines.

Fold

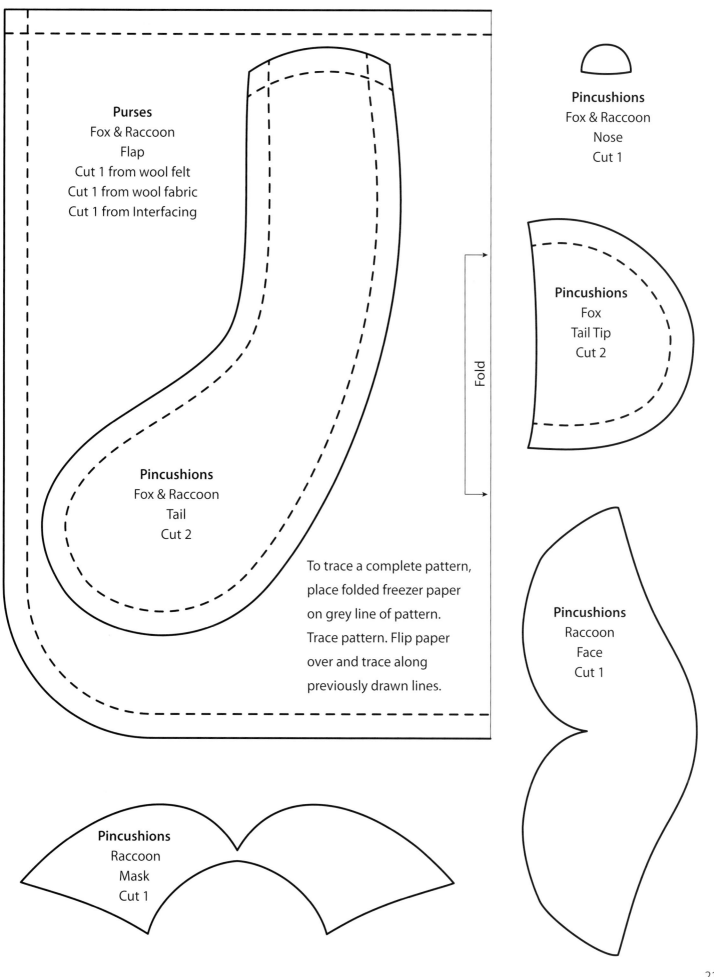

Purses
Fox & Raccoon
Flap
Cut 1 from wool felt
Cut 1 from wool fabric
Cut 1 from Interfacing

Pincushions
Fox & Raccoon
Nose
Cut 1

Pincushions
Fox
Tail Tip
Cut 2

Fold

Pincushions
Fox & Raccoon
Tail
Cut 2

To trace a complete pattern, place folded freezer paper on grey line of pattern. Trace pattern. Flip paper over and trace along previously drawn lines.

Pincushions
Raccoon
Face
Cut 1

Pincushions
Raccoon
Mask
Cut 1

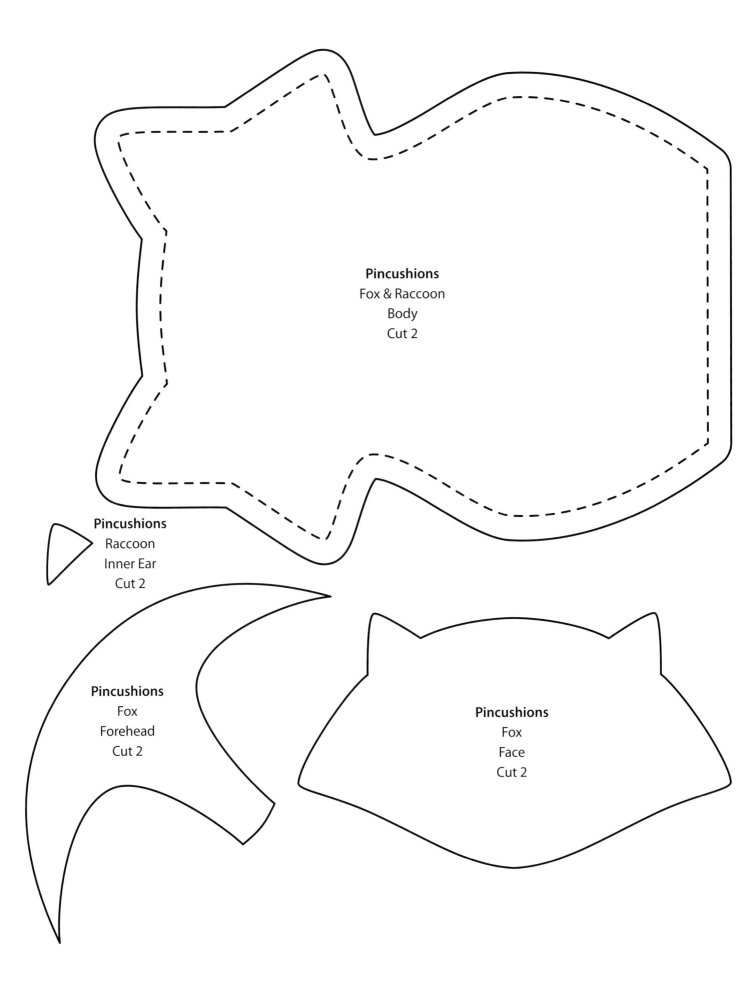

Pincushions
Fox & Raccoon
Body
Cut 2

Pincushions
Raccoon
Inner Ear
Cut 2

Pincushions
Fox
Forehead
Cut 2

Pincushions
Fox
Face
Cut 2

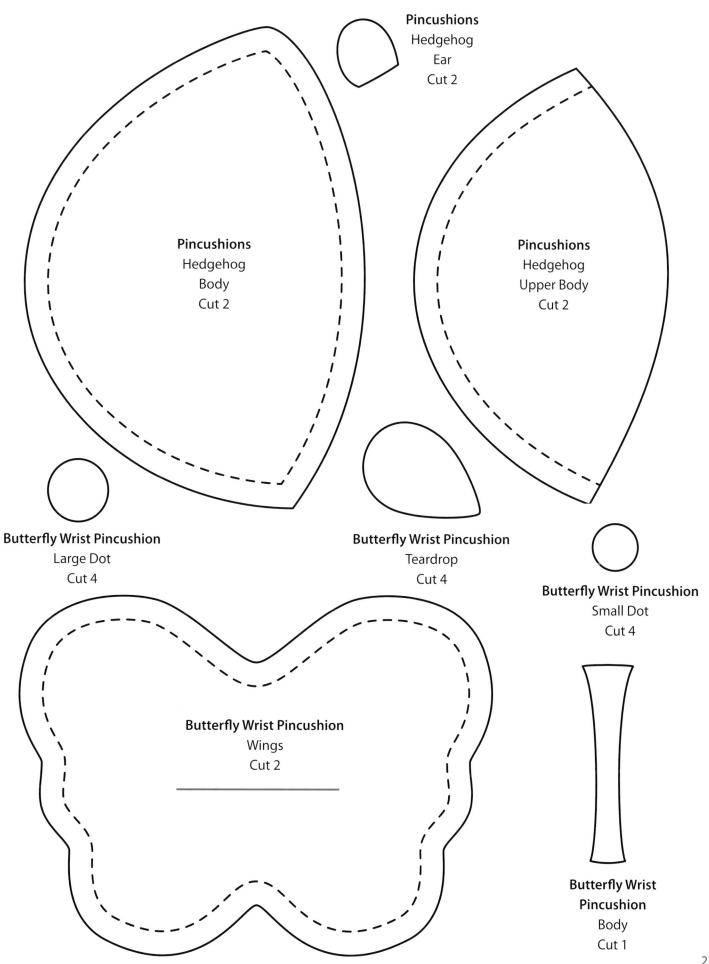

Pincushions
Hedgehog
Ear
Cut 2

Pincushions
Hedgehog
Body
Cut 2

Pincushions
Hedgehog
Upper Body
Cut 2

Butterfly Wrist Pincushion
Large Dot
Cut 4

Butterfly Wrist Pincushion
Teardrop
Cut 4

Butterfly Wrist Pincushion
Small Dot
Cut 4

Butterfly Wrist Pincushion
Wings
Cut 2

Butterfly Wrist
Pincushion
Body
Cut 1

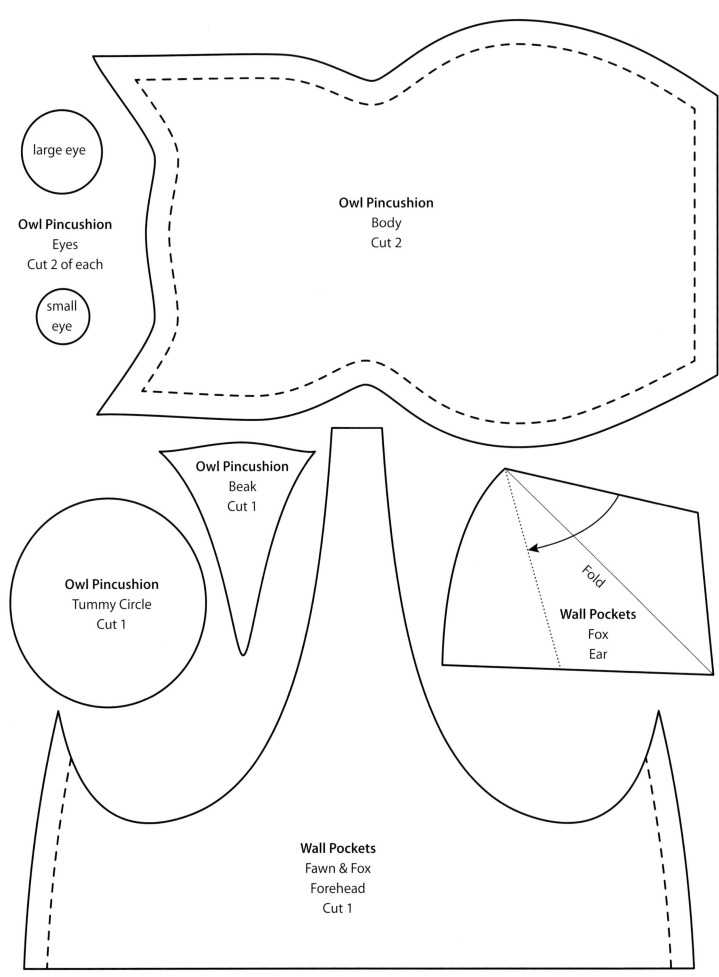

large eye

Owl Pincushion
Eyes
Cut 2 of each

small
eye

Owl Pincushion
Body
Cut 2

Owl Pincushion
Beak
Cut 1

Owl Pincushion
Tummy Circle
Cut 1

Fold

Wall Pockets
Fox
Ear

Wall Pockets
Fawn & Fox
Forehead
Cut 1

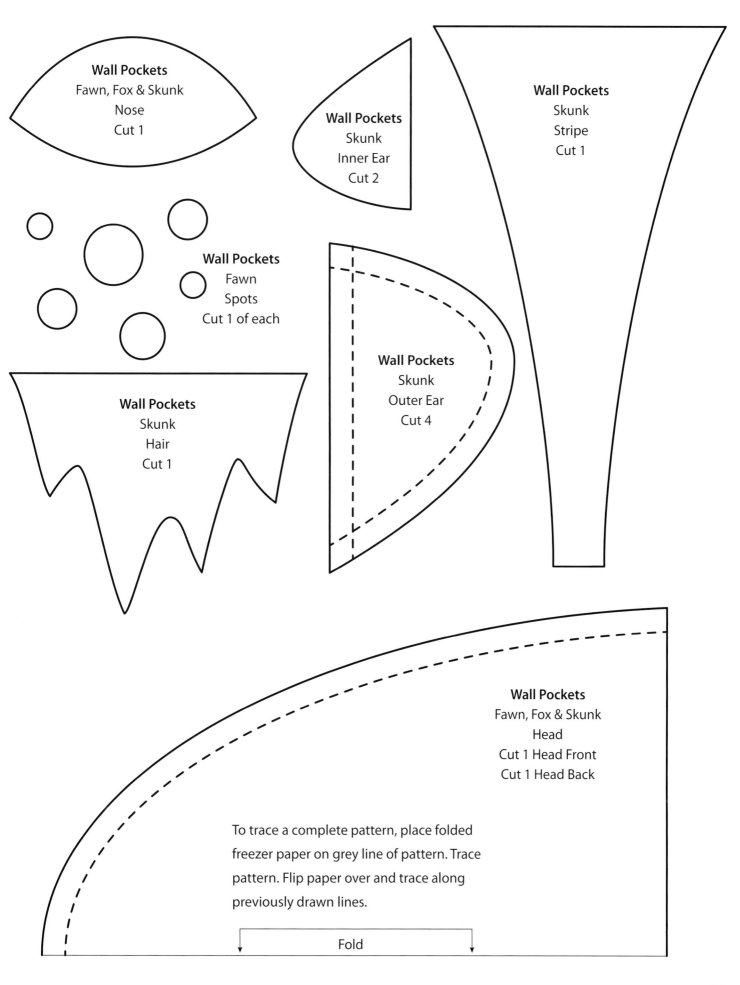

Wall Pockets
Fawn, Fox & Skunk
Nose
Cut 1

Wall Pockets
Skunk
Inner Ear
Cut 2

Wall Pockets
Skunk
Stripe
Cut 1

Wall Pockets
Fawn
Spots
Cut 1 of each

Wall Pockets
Skunk
Hair
Cut 1

Wall Pockets
Skunk
Outer Ear
Cut 4

Wall Pockets
Fawn, Fox & Skunk
Head
Cut 1 Head Front
Cut 1 Head Back

To trace a complete pattern, place folded freezer paper on grey line of pattern. Trace pattern. Flip paper over and trace along previously drawn lines.

Fold

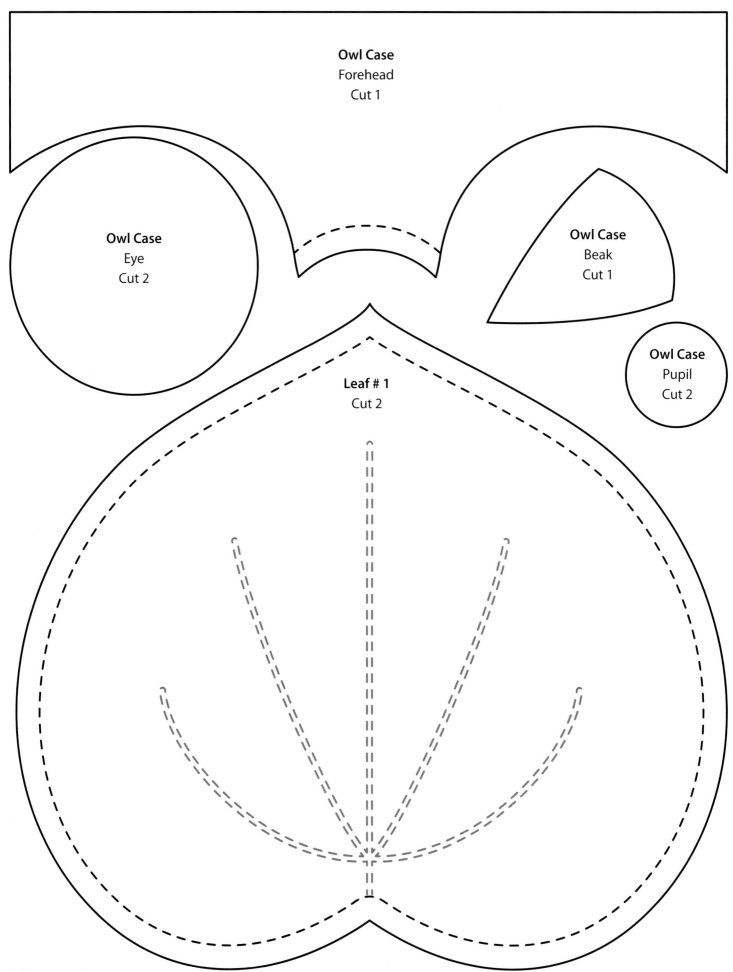

Owl Case
Forehead
Cut 1

Owl Case
Eye
Cut 2

Owl Case
Beak
Cut 1

Owl Case
Pupil
Cut 2

Leaf # 1
Cut 2

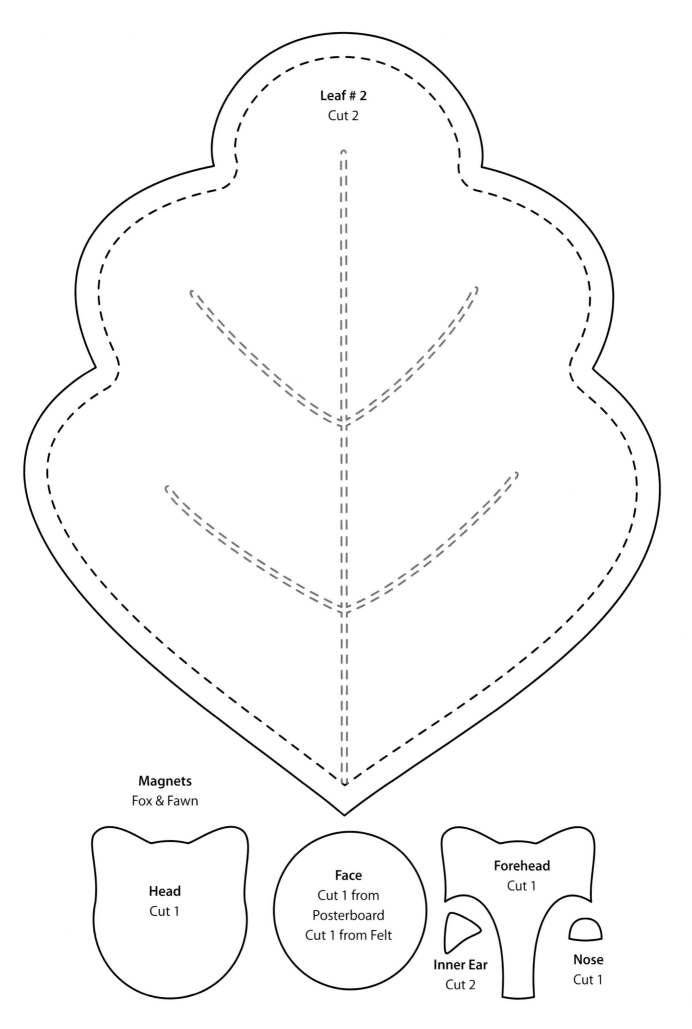

Leaf # 2
Cut 2

Magnets
Fox & Fawn

Head
Cut 1

Face
Cut 1 from
Posterboard
Cut 1 from Felt

Forehead
Cut 1

Inner Ear
Cut 2

Nose
Cut 1

27

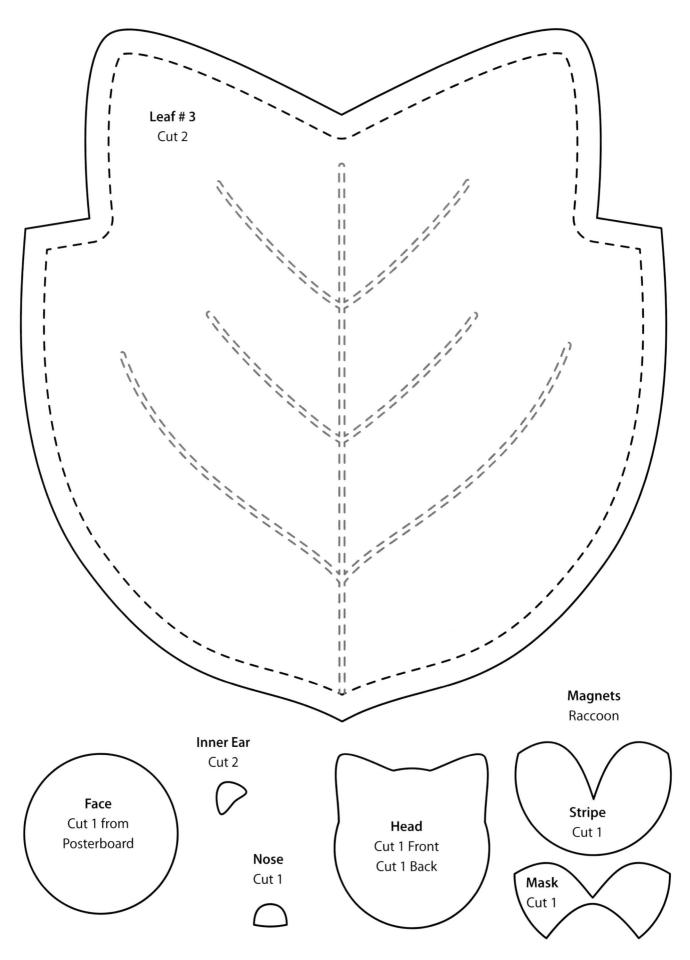

Leaf # 3
Cut 2

Face
Cut 1 from
Posterboard

Inner Ear
Cut 2

Nose
Cut 1

Head
Cut 1 Front
Cut 1 Back

Magnets
Raccoon

Stripe
Cut 1

Mask
Cut 1

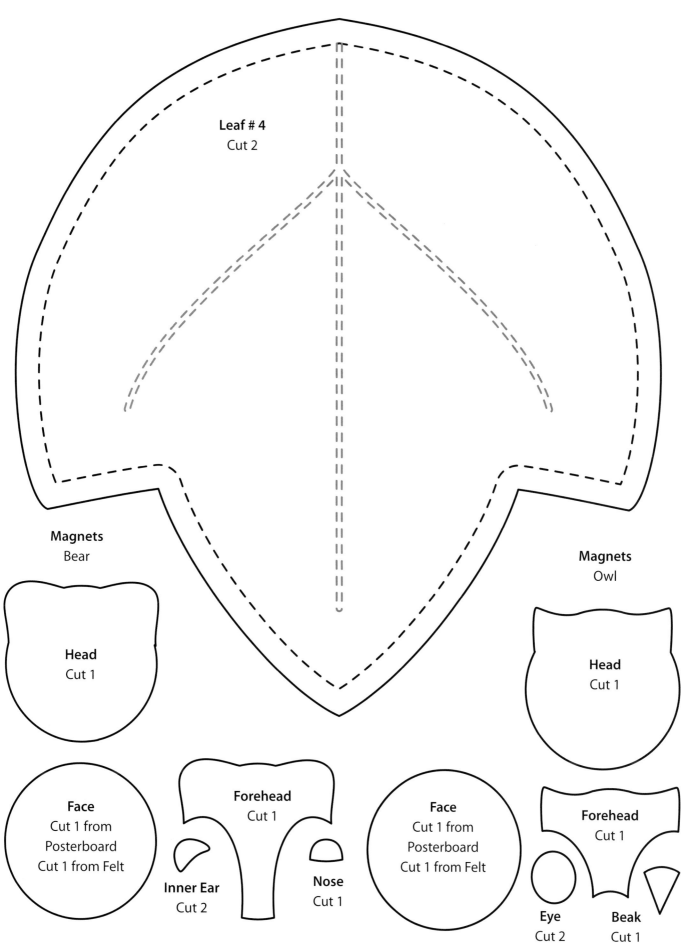

Leaf # 4
Cut 2

Magnets
Bear

Head
Cut 1

Magnets
Owl

Head
Cut 1

Face
Cut 1 from
Posterboard
Cut 1 from Felt

Forehead
Cut 1

Inner Ear
Cut 2

Nose
Cut 1

Face
Cut 1 from
Posterboard
Cut 1 from Felt

Forehead
Cut 1

Eye
Cut 2

Beak
Cut 1

General Instructions

FELTED WOOL

Felted wool is woven wool fabric that is washed in hot soapy water, rinsed in cold water and dried in a hot clothes dryer causing the fabric to shrink by about 10-20%. Felting wool is a handy technique to use when a patterned fabric is needed, like the grey and black stripe used for the Raccoon Pincushion's tail, page 10.

WOOL FELT

Wool felt is made from wool fibers or a combination of wool and other fibers that have been compressed into a material that does not fray or ravel. Wool felt comes in 100% wool and wool blends. The wool felt used for most of these projects is a wool/rayon blend. It is not necessary to prewash or preshrink wool felt.

DYEING WOOL

Wool felt or wool felt blends that contain at least 85% wool can be dyed using *unsweetened* powdered soft drink mix (Kool-Aid® or a similar product) or food color tablets (the type used for dyeing eggs). After dyeing, the color is permanent.

Dyeing with food color tablets provides lots of color options. You can use a single color to add a subtle mottled variation to the original wool felt color, different intensities of similar colors to add a marbled effect, or multiple colors to add a dramatic flair.

Starting with a colored wool will add subtle variation when using darker shades of the fabric color like the Log Storage Case leaf on page 18. Starting with white wool will produce clearer, truer color.

Using Powdered Soft Drink Mix

- For a deep, rich color for about a 9" square of wool, mix about $1/2$ cup of water with 1 package of drink mix in a glass bowl. For a lighter color, add more water. **Note:** You might want to test the color on a small scrap of wool fabric before dyeing your entire piece. For larger pieces of wool use 1 additional package of drink mix and $1/2$ cup of water for each additional 9" square of fabric.

- Soak the fabric in warm soapy water (use a small squirt of dishwashing liquid) for about 20 minutes.

- Rinse the pre-soaked wool piece in warm clear water; remove. Place the wet wool piece in a microwave-safe glass dish.

- Use a sponge-type brush or a spoon to apply the dye to the wool. This will give you a marbled effect like the **Butterfly Wrist Pincushion**, page 7. You can use multiple colors of dye to add more interest, if desired.

- Making sure the wool is very wet (add more water if needed), microwave on low for 1-2 minutes, allow to rest for 1-2 minutes. Repeat once or twice. Only the dye will move into the wool, leaving clear water remaining in the bowl.

Using Food Color Tablets

Mix the tablets with vinegar following the manufacturer's instructions. Follow **Using Powdered Soft Drink Mix**, left, to complete the dyeing process.

MAKING & USING PATTERNS
Tracing Paper Patterns

Trace the patterns onto tracing paper, being sure to transfer all markings; cut out. Pin the patterns to the corresponding fabric pieces. Cut out the fabric shapes. Reuse paper patterns as needed to cut the number of pieces needed for your project.

Freezer Paper Patterns

With the paper (dull) side facing up and allowing about $1/2$" between shapes, trace the patterns onto freezer paper. Make 1 pattern for each piece needed. Rough-cut the patterns apart. With the plastic (shiny) side down, use a warm, dry iron to press each piece onto the corresponding fabric pieces. Cut out the fabric shapes along the drawn lines. Remove the freezer paper. Freeze paper patterns can be used more than once.

Rotary Cutting

Cutting Cotton Fabric:
- Place the fabric on your work surface with the fold closest to you.

- Cut all strips from the selvage-to-selvage width of the fabric unless otherwise indicated in the project instructions.

- Square the left edge of the fabric using the rotary cutter and rulers *(Figs. 1-2)*.

Fig. 1	Fig. 2
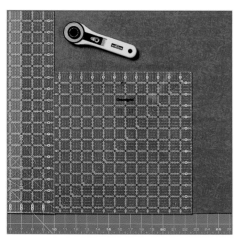	

- To cut each strip required for a project, place ruler over the cut edge of the fabric, aligning the desired marking on the ruler with the cut edge; make the cut *(Fig. 3)*.

Fig. 3

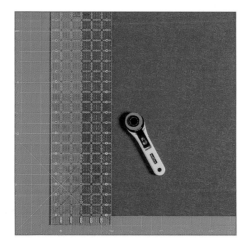

- When cutting several strips from a single piece of fabric, it is important that the cuts remain at a perfect right angle to the fold; square fabric as needed.

Cutting Wool Felt:
- Place a single layer of wool felt on your work surface.

- Square the left edge of the wool felt using the rotary cutter and rulers as shown in Figs. 1-2.

- Place ruler over the cut edge of the wool felt, aligning the desired marking on the ruler with the cut edge; make the cut.

Sewing and Pressing
- Begin with a new needle (size 70 or 80) in your machine. Set the machine stitch length to either 2.5 or 3 (11 or 9 stitches per inch, respectively). Clean the bobbin casing regularly as you sew to remove the lint that might accumulate there.

- Use general purpose thread in the bobbin and the needle. Match the thread color to the felt color or choose a contrasting color.

- When pressing wool felt, use a dry iron and the wool setting.

- When fusing wool felt, follow the fusible web manufacturer's instructions for using their product.

- When pressing cotton fabrics, use the cotton setting.

Embroidery

Use embroidery (chenille) needles and # 5, # 8, or #12 pearl cotton for all embroidery. The higher the number, the finer the thread. The eye of the needle should be large enough to easily thread the pearl cotton and the shaft needs to make a large enough hole in the felt to avoid drag on the pearl cotton.
• Size 18 needle for #5 pearl cotton
• Size 20 needle for #8 pearl cotton
• Size 22 needle for #12 pearl cotton

Blanket Stitch

Bring the thread up from the wrong side. Working to the right, place the needle as shown, stitching into the felt (Fig. 4). Keeping the thread below the point of the needle go down at 2 and come up at 3 and tug gently to close the stitch. Continue working in the same manner, going down at even numbers and coming up at odd numbers (Fig. 5).

Fig. 4

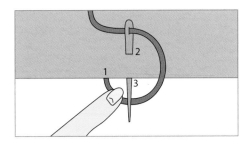

Fig. 5

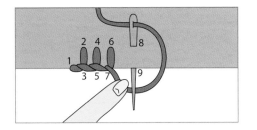

Cross Stitch

Come up at 1 and go down at 2.
Come up at 3 and go down at 4.

Fig. 6

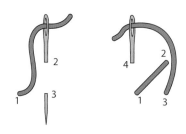

Outline Stitch

Come up at 1. Keeping the thread above the stitching line, go down at 2 and come up at 3 (Fig. 7). Continue working in the same manner, keeping the stitches a consistent length.

Fig. 7

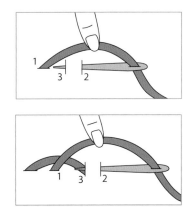

Running Stitch

Come up at 1 and go down at 2.
Come up at 3 and go down at 4.
Continue working in the same manner, keeping the stitches a consistent length.

Fig. 8

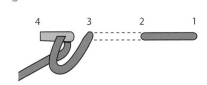

Straight Stitch

"Stab" the needle straight up and down through the felt. Come up at 1, go down at 2. Continue working in the same manner to complete the number of stitches needed. (Fig. 9).

Fig. 9

Production Team: Technical Writers – Mary Hutcheson, Lisa Lancaster, and Jean Lewis; Editorial Writer – Susan Frantz Wiles; Senior Graphic Artist – Lora Puls; Graphic Artist – Frances Huddleston; Photostylist – Lori Wenger; Photographer –Jason Masters.